The Wedding Book of Calm

G000091125

from confetti.co.uk
don't get married without us…

First published in 2001 by Octopus Publishing Group,
2–4 Heron Quays, London E14 4JP
www.conran-octopus.co.uk
Reprinted in 2003, 2004, 2005 (twice)

ISBN 1 84091 223 5

Publishing Director Lorraine Dickey;
Creative Director Leslie Harrington;
Senior Editor Katey Day; *Copy-editor* Helen Ridge;
Designer Megan Smith; *Production Director* Zoë Fawcett

Contents

Is planning your wedding bringing you out
in a cold sweat, or are you waking up in
the middle of the night panicking about
whether you ordered the right shade
of ribbon for the bridesmaids' petticoats?
Then you need to remember that this
is meant to be the best day of your
life – and fun!

INTRODUCTION

Confetti.co.uk has taken the stress out of wedding planning for thousands of couples (as well as for their wedding party and guests). Here you can read the advice they and other brides have found holds the key to a successful, painless wedding.

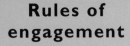

Rules of engagement

Simply the best

Crikey, you're getting married! Before those wedding plans spiral out of control, remember that the more complex the plans, the more stressful life's going to be. So keep it simple.

Make a list

Writing things down may seem boring, but it's a top way of remembering everything. And think of the sense of achievement you'll feel when you tick off each task.

It's in the timing

Leaving things until the last minute is asking for trouble, so get the 'biggies' – legal, financial and religious matters – out of the way first. Once they're booked and sorted, you can start to breathe again.

Set your priorities

Decide what really matters most to
you about your wedding. Is it the cake?
The dress? The venue? Once you've
established that, you can gauge exactly
how much time and effort you want
to spend on each aspect.

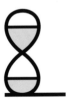

Take a recce...
Before booking the entertainment, check
out their act. Your wedding day isn't the
ideal moment to discover that the whole
band is tone-deaf!

Chill out

It's all so exciting and important, but don't let your wedding arrangements take over your life. Put aside a little chunk of time daily to do, um, nothing.

Think small

Sure, every detail of your wedding has to be just right. But the first step to staying calm is not to fret over small issues. And step two is to treat all issues as small issues.

Rome wasn't built...

It's tempting to think you can organize everything in a weekend – but don't! Allow yourself a buffer zone between planning each stage. You'll be so much calmer and you'll enjoy yourself much more along the way.

The twilight zone

Not everyone's at their sparky best first
thing in the morning. Choose the time
when you feel most awake and efficient to
make those all-important preparations –
even if it is the middle of the night.

Don't panic, don't panic!
The quickest way to get into a state is to
worry about what's going to happen next.
So forget the future and focus on what's
going on NOW.

Trash the trivia

Don't get hung up on the small stuff. Do you really think people care whether the bridesmaids' shoes match the table decorations?

Ditch the details

Weddings don't have to follow a set pattern, so don't add to your workload by trying to incorporate details you couldn't care less about. If you don't want a 'theme' or a 'colour', for example, then simply don't have one!

Get a life

Remember the way you had a life before
you started this wedding business? Try
getting it back – even if it is for only half an
hour each day.

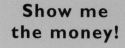

Show me
the money!

Target your wedge!

Decide where you want to spend most of your money. For instance, if it's on the reception, allocate your funds accordingly, and cut back on other things that matter less to you, such as the wedding invitations.

How much?

Set a budget for your wedding and stick to it. It might sound stuffy, but it's better than the spectre of your bank manager hanging over you at the wedding.

SHOW ME THE MONEY!

Money talks...
But that's not much cop if nobody else does. Conflicts over money aren't uncommon, so sort out who's paying for what, and why, from the outset. Working out finances calmly and clearly can prevent a lot of problems later on.

Learn to negotiate

If something you want is too expensive,
negotiate. And if you can't get the price you
want, shrug and walk away. You will find
what you're looking for at the right price
eventually.

It's a wonderful life

Don't obsess about not having enough
money for the wedding you want. Instead,
focus on what you can afford – and go all
out to get it!

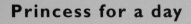

Princess for a day

Plan ahead

For a dream day, you need a dream wedding dress. This is probably the most important element of your big day, so give yourself plenty of time to track down the right one.

Designs on you

Finding the right wedding dress is a daunting prospect. The sheer choice of dresses can bring even the most balanced girl out in a sweat, so take your time, flick through lots of magazines and check out the confetti.co.uk website for inspiration.

Enlist a friend

Don't forget the fun factor when you're dress-hunting. When you're ready to start trying on dresses, take a friend whose opinion you value and trust, and play 'dressing up' for the day!

Shop around

Keep an organized and updated list of any bargain stores that you hear about. When the time comes to buy, you could pick up the wedding shoes or bridesmaids' gifts at a fraction of the original cost.

Zips, trains and veils

Keep in mind the practicalities. A dress
that has lots of zips, buttons and hooks
may seem sexy now, but remember that
not only are you going to have to get
the dress on – your fiancé is going to
have to get it off again!

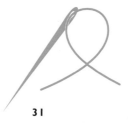

Going undercover

Brides often get their underwear wrong.
Tight-fitting push-up bras and stomach-
flattening knickers may seem like a godsend
at the start of the day, but such flesh-
restricting options can seriously jeopardize
your comfort.

Do or diet

All brides want to look perfect on their big day, but don't be tempted to crash-diet. It's not only bad for your health, but it will also zap your energy and leave you looking tired and run-down.

Hair today

Your nuptials may not be the best time to try out a radical new hairstyle – the last thing you need is a bad hair day at your wedding. If you do want something different, get your hair restyled in advance – so if anything goes wrong it can be remedied before you get hitched.

Forget the bridesmaids!

While it's important for the bridesmaids to feel comfortable in their dresses, don't feel selfish about choosing outfits that you want them to wear. This is NOT the time to put other people first.

Made-up

When it comes to make-up, keep it simple. Remember, it's going to be a long day, with lots of laughter and probably a few tears. You don't want to be running to the loo to powder your nose every half an hour.

You're gorgeous, you are

Everyone has days when they don't feel great about themselves, but try not to let any negative feelings take over in the run-up to your wedding. You're a special person and you will look beautiful on your big day – so believe it!

And you are who?

Remember that bloke you're going to marry? Don't forget to include him when you're making decisions. And even if he doesn't want to get involved with all the arrangements, make sure he knows you still value his ideas.

Never mind the napkins

Keep things in perspective. The colour of the napkins really isn't important in the greater scheme of things. What does matter is that you're marrying the man you want to spend the rest of your life with.

Hubbies and hobbies

Being a couple is about doing things
together, not just arranging a wedding. Think
about new hobbies or skills you'd like to
learn together when the big day is simply a
distant memory.

Fancy a quick one...?

Boost of energy, that is. Ginseng is good for kick-starting the system, and it's also reputed to soothe frayed nerves when taken regularly.

Borrow the best man

Enlist the help of the best man to either
get him interested in the planning
or to take him down the pub when you
need to focus on the bits he finds boring!

Walk away

Gearing up for a prenuptial slanging match?
Before you come to blows, go for a short,
brisk walk. When you return in a calmer
frame of mind, then have your say.

He's the man

Just because he isn't interested in the colour of the confetti or the bridesmaids' outfits doesn't mean that he doesn't care about the wedding – or you.

Together forever

It's not just your wedding you've got to look forward to – it's the rest of your lives together. So keep things in perspective by looking ahead at all the wonderful times you're going to share.

Forget the wedding!

Not literally, of course, but take time out to
have a couple of wedding-free days when
you talk about anything BUT the big day.

Chuck your watch

Liberate yourself and leave your watch at
home. It's amazing how relaxed you'll feel
when you remove the pressure of time.

Keep still

Stop running around for a minute. Notice anything – like how all that tension starts slipping away and your body and mind feel instantly relaxed?

Love lavender

Adding a few drops of lavender essential oil to your evening bath is a wonderful de-stresser. Use an aromatherapy burner to release the calming fragrance, or put a few drops on your pillow to help you sleep at night.

Brighten up

Look on the bright side of life. Turn problems into 'challenges' and nerves into 'excitement'. Use the positive power of words to keep you calm.

Save the rant

When someone asks how you are, don't rant on about how preoccupied you are with the wedding preparations. It may be true, but there's more to your life than that. Focus on other things that are happening and you'll actually feel less stressed than you thought.

Live for the moment

Most worries centre on what may happen
in the future. But nine times out of ten
nothing ever comes of them. And, since
you've planned everything so well, focus
on the present – the future will take
care of itself.

Muscle missy

Feeling tense? Find a comfy spot, lie down
and close your eyes. Visualize your muscles
and relax them one by one until your
whole body feels soothed.

Be alert

Usually there will be a warning signal to let you know it's time to slow down and take a breather. Look out for the signs and you can avoid chaos before it hits you head on.

Scream and scream again

Bottling up your emotions is never the answer. Relieve tension with a good old cry or simply allow yourself to scream. How good does that feel?

Magic words

Try affirmations to put you in a positive mood. Choose a simple phrase, such as 'Every day I'm getting closer to the wedding I want,' and repeat it whenever you feel down or apprehensive.

Snoozeville

Get enough sleep. It's vital to be rested if you want to be relaxed, so don't organize and agonize into the night. Get your head down at a reasonable time every evening.

Share the load

Lots of women have been through the bridal experience, so get them to share their stories with you. It'll make you feel better when you hear that everything worked out OK for them in the end.

Picture perfect

Visualization is a vital stress-reliever. Create
a mental picture of your perfect wedding.
Seeing everything going so well will remind
you that your wedding will be perfect in
real life, too.

Tap into stress

Tap in to the relaxing acupressure points
on your head by simply washing your hair,
or even just mimicking the action.

Forgive and forget

Arguments happen. For an instant
tension-buster put two drops of Bach's
Beech Flower remedy under your tongue.
It's thought to help resolve bitterness and
anger and stop you being overcritical.

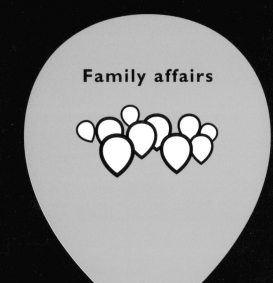

Rent-a-crowd

It's going to be impossible to do everything
yourself, so delegate. Don't worry about
burdening friends and family – they'll be
only too delighted to help – but be very
specific about what you want others to do.

Honesty is the best policy
Whatever your parents want, remember
that it's your wedding. The sooner they
realize you're going to do things your way,
the more time they'll have to come around
to your way of thinking.

Slug it out

Arguments will happen – just make sure
they're not left to fester. Get any
differences of opinion out in the open and
you won't have guests with a grudge on
your wedding day.

Repeat after me...

If a family meeting is sending your blood pressure sky-high, repeat this phrase: 'Every moment I feel calmer and calmer.' Say it often enough and your subconscious will begin to believe it!

It's good to talk

Bottling up resentment never does any
good, and any lingering negative feelings will
simply cause stress on your wedding day –
so keep the lines of communication open.

Let it go

Your mum says something that really annoys you, but let it go. Why? Remind yourself that it's your reaction to the comment, not the comment itself, that affects your state of calm.

Please yourself

Remember: you can't please all of the people all of the time. For once in your life, don't get stressed out over appearing selfish.

Split scenes

Dealing with divorced parents can be tricky, but getting them in the same room on the same day can be done. Just make sure that you've worked out the strategy in advance and that both parties are in agreement.

Give and take

Much as you want everything to be done
your way, there will be times when
you'll be forced to compromise. Instead
of fighting it, accept the fact and you'll feel
a whole lot calmer.

Food for thought

Veg out!

Use your diet to help you beat stress.
Eat plenty of wholegrain foods and around
five portions of fresh fruit and veg every
day. For an extra energy boost, snack
on a banana.

Sup on a smoothie

Throw your favourite fruits into the blender and whizz them up on the highest setting. This makes a delicious fruit cocktail and will give you bags of energy.

Can the caffeine

Coffee, tea and cola-type drinks might give you an instant high, but too much caffeine will raise your stress levels and keep you up at night. Switch to calming camomile tea instead.

Water therapy

Drink plenty of water — aim for two litres a day. Your health will improve, your skin will glow and you'll boost your feelings of calm.

Milk it

Milk is wonderfully calming. It contains calcium, which relaxes the muscles, and an amino acid called tryptophan, which is a potent natural sedative.

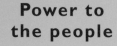

Power to
the people

You decide

Prepare to be surrounded by experts —
from the florist to the caterer to the
hairdresser — who will all want to tell you
what they think you need for the ideal
wedding. Listen to their advice, but
remember that you and your partner
are the ultimate decision-makers.

Breathing space

If you feel under pressure, don't make an immediate decision. Explain that you need more time before giving your final answer.

Go with your intuition

Something about the wedding arrangements feels wrong? Go with your gut instinct and you'll feel back in control – and calmer.

Mind the tact

Don't be bullied into agreeing to something you're uncomfortable with. A tactful refusal to an offer is all that's needed, for example, 'I appreciate what you're saying, but I would like the simpler menu.'

Don't throw a wobbly

Don't have 'It's my day!' tantrums every time someone tries to help. Most people really do have your best interests at heart, so listen to what they have to say. Who knows, it might even be useful!

Deflect stress

Learn to spot those occasions when you're absorbing someone else's tension. Visualize an imaginary line between you and the other person, and picture their stress bouncing off the boundary and missing you altogether.

Stand up for yourself

Be assertive. Although you'll have to make some compromises, your wedding is no time to be a people-pleaser. Make what you want clear from the start, and be honest about any suggestions you don't like.

A friend in need

There's no doubt that organizing a wedding
can be stressful, and friends could end up
taking the flak when your plans don't quite
work out. Give them advance warning that
things could get tricky and ask them to cut
you a little slack for a while.

Trust others

It isn't your job to worry about how each
guest is going to get to the wedding.
Provide them with maps and any
information they need to find the venue,
and trust them to get there. They will!

Treat yourself!

A bit of indulgence

Pamper yourself with a day at a health club.
What could be more relaxing than a swim,
sauna and steam room session? Take a
friend along for some girly chat while you
wind down.

Dolly daydream

Take time out to daydream. Let your mind
wander and you'll be surprised how quickly
solutions pop into your head.

Be lazy

Instead of traipsing around town to find your dress, florist, venue, invitations and party decorations, log onto confetti.co.uk and organise your wedding without even leaving home.

Female bonding

Friends are fantastic when you're feeling stressed. Get yours together for a big night out (before the hen night) and give yourself a giggle.

Be a daredy-cat

If making the smallest decision sets your mind in a tailspin, it's time to do something completely different. A bungee jump or a spot of abseiling should help you shake off your pre-wedding blues.

Feet first

Traipsing around shops can leave you tense and worn out. Soak your feet in warm water, then massage with a moisturiser or a blend of relaxing essential oils. Bliss!

Sleep easy

If stress is keeping you awake at night and your mind is busy with wedding plans, try a couple of drops of the White Chestnut remedy from the Bach flower collection.

Rub-a-dub

A long soak in a warm bath is an instant
soother. Surround yourself with candlelight,
add a few drops of your favourite essential
oil and float away on a sea of calm. No
rubber duck required!

Touchy-feely

Massage is a wonderful way to relax. Add a few drops of your favourite aromatherapy oil to the massage oil, to boost its effectiveness.

The final countdown...

Put the brakes on...

There's only so much organizing you can do. Give yourself a deadline to complete the arrangements two or three days before the wedding – then stop!

Time it right

Draw up a timetable for the wedding morning. Knowing exactly how long you've got to get ready, have your hair done, pick up the flowers and do all the other little jobs should help you avoid a last-minute rush.

Bin the booze

On the eve of your wedding, resist the temptation to drink too much to calm your nerves – one glass of wine should do. After all, you want to wake up feeling fresh as a daisy, not horribly hung over.

Flower power

Brides swear by Rescue Remedy, a homeopathic flower tincture. Just put a few drops on your tongue as and when you feel anxious or panicky. Natural remedies such as kava kava work a treat, too.

Be realistic

However hard you've worked, bear in mind that life never goes exactly according to plan. If you prepare yourself mentally for a little disappointment, then any minor glitches shouldn't spoil your enjoyment on the day.

Ease into it

Begin the big day as calmly as possible by making sure your timetable allows for a long soak in the bath and a cup of tea. That way you should feel nice and serene when it's time to get dressed.

Bridal breakfast

Even if you have butterflies in your tummy,
eat something for breakfast to avoid feeling
faint later on. Some cereal or a piece of
toast will do.

Avoid stimulants

Tempting as it is to have a wake-up cup of coffee with a couple of reviving sugars – don't! These stimulants will set your pulse racing and blow away any feelings of calm.

Busy bodies

There are bound to be people around you who are driving you nuts! Get them out of your hair by delegating little jobs to them.

Beauty business

No bride wants the trauma of getting make-up or nail varnish on her dress, so get ready in the right order. Do your manicure and face first, then put the dress on — carefully! That way, you're sure to stay composed.

Quick clean-ups

Beauticians will tell you that much of the art of putting on make-up lies in how quickly and effectively you can correct your mistakes. Keep cleanser and cotton wool buds handy so that you can wipe away that splodge of eyeliner in a flash.

Stay centred

Keep calm by focusing your attention on
the present. Don't even think about
whether your fiancé has arrived at the
church or if the best man has the ring.

Every breath you take...
Focus on your breath. If you're breathing
rapidly, take deep, slow breaths, listening to
each breath as it comes and goes. That
should calm you down.

Brow-beaters

It's going to be a hectic day. Help soothe
away tension by first stroking your forehead
firmly with your fingers and gradually
moving to the back of your head.

Say 'Ommmm...'

Sit quietly and hum very gently. The hum
will resonate through your body and soon
lighten your mood.

Talk positively

Positive self-talk sends a command to your subconscious, helping your affirmations become a reality. Try saying over and over again to yourself, 'I am calm, focused and in control.'

Look ahead

Being the centre of attention all day can be quite wearing. Take a moment to look away from your audience – focusing on a distant object is instantly relaxing.

Act up

If you act calm and imagine that everyone
around you sees you as a chilled-out
person, in next to no time you'll become
that person.

Get loved-up

As you enter the wedding venue, remember that everyone there wishes you well and wants the very best for you and your husband-to-be. Use their feelings of love and goodwill to soothe your nerves.

Hold the champagne
Don't get completely sloshed at the
reception. Your wedding day is something
to remember for the rest of your life –
you don't want it to disappear in an
alcoholic blur.

Mum's the word

When the celebration is over, leave it to your mum to settle any outstanding arrangements, such as the safekeeping of presents and allocating any leftover cake.

Have a cry

A good cry can be emotionally and physically soothing, so don't be afraid to let out a few tears.

Treat your face

Getting married is tiring. Soak away any
facial tension with a hot, damp face towel.

Look to the sun

Finding it hard to come down?
Picture a setting sun – you'll find it
incredibly soothing.

Smile

After such a big day, you're bound to feel a little drained. Take a moment to look around you and smile – you're married!

ABOUT CONFETTI.CO.UK

Confetti.co.uk is the UK's leading wedding and special occasion website, helping more than 100,000 brides, grooms and guests every month.

To find out more or to order your confetti.co.uk gift book or party brochure, visit www.confetti.co.uk, call 0870 840 6060, or e-mail us at info@confetti.co.uk

Other books in this series include *Wedding Readings*; *Men at Weddings*; *Compatibility*; *Confettiquette*; *Speeches* and the comprehensive *Wedding Planner*.